TABLE OF CON

INTRODUCTION..4

ADMISSIONS 5

    Admissions Tips 8

    Admissions Definitions 9

FINANCIAL AID 17

    Financial Aid Tips 20

    Financial Aid Definitions 21

COLLEGIATE ATHLETIC ASSOCIATIONS 26

    NCAA 28

    NJCAA 30

    NAIA 32

RECRUITING DEFINITIONS 35

DIVING INTO THE NCAA 39

    Core Courses 40

    Eligibility Center 42

    Certification Decisions 43

    Division I 44

    Division II 48

    Division III 52

    Contact Rules 54

THE COLLEGE RECRUITING PROCESS 57

    The College Recruiting Project 58

    Things to Consider 59

    Yearly Tasks 60

    Contacting Coaches 62

    Recruiting Video 65

    Campus Visit 69

    Questions to Ask 73

PARENTS' ROLE 78

WHAT DO I NEED 80

RECRUITING SERVICES 83

    Do It Yourself (DIY)...84

    Personal Recruiters 85

    Traditional Recruiting Services....................................85

THE BESEENSPORTS METHOD 87

About the Authors

Leah Bernier, Head Coach

A 2-time team captain, 2-time team MVP and AVCA All-Region Selection at the NCAA Division I level, Leah Bernier was an accomplished student-athlete that has taken her love of playing and turned it into a successful coaching career. The 2001 America East Conference Player of the Year, Leah has coached at almost every level from middle school to NCAA Division 1. Her love of working with student-athletes and giving them the tools to be successful in life was a driving force in developing a book to help more people achieve collegiate goals.

With a wealth of experience coaching volleyball and recruiting student-athletes over the last 16 years, Leah has guided multiple teams to success while helping individual student-athletes along their journey. Leah knows the complete college recruiting process and is tested by the NCAA every year.

Over the years, Leah has witnessed the struggles that families endure to help their student-athletes play their sport in college while getting a meaningful education. Part of that struggle is paying a lot of money for things they can do themselves if they only had the information on how to do it. This spurred Leah to write this book and help families save money by doing the crucial work themselves. This book was born from Leah's desire to remove the noise from the college recruiting process and present the process in a factual form.

Eddie Johnson, PMP

A certified Project Manager with over 20 years' experience, Eddie is the Managing Director of Rebel Visions Corporation and founder of BeSeenSports™. Putting his project management experience to practical use, Eddie and his team built BeSeenSports™ to provide people with the tools they need to successfully navigate the college recruiting journey. Named by Eddie's son, the platform was created to respond to what seemed to be an overly costly and confusing college recruiting industry.

Attending a major volleyball tournament in Washington, D.C., Eddie was introduced to Leah and an immediate friendship was born. Both sharing their mutual desire to remove the mysticism from the college recruiting process while simplifying the journey. Making the dream of playing sports in college an attainable goal for almost anyone willing to put in the work.

The pairing of Leah's knowledge and experience and Eddie's project management approach to the journey are a natural fit and provide people with the facts and an actionable approach to completing this impacting life decision.

COLLEGE Admissions

FINDING THE RIGHT COLLEGE CAN BE A BIG CHALLENGE.

Your college recruiting work truly begins in 8th grade. Although these grades do not count toward your official high school transcript, they do set the tone for your high school career. The grades you get during your 8th year set your path for your high school freshman year. Do well, and you can get into Honors classes or even Advanced Placement (AP) classes. Do poorly, and you can find yourself starting your high school career behind the curve.

The college admissions process **continues your freshmen year of high school** when every grade you earn becomes part of your official transcript. That transcript is what college admission counselors will use to determine whether or not you fit their academic profile and qualify for admission to their school. **The better your grades, the more schools you will have to choose from!**

By the time you are a sophomore, you also need to make sure that you are paying close attention to the TYPES of classes you are taking and how successful you can be at them. AP and Honors courses help with getting into high academic schools, but you also have to do well in those courses to make it count!

Also, looking into your sophomore and junior year, you will need to start working on **THE TESTS!** The SAT and/or ACT tests are often required by most colleges. Sometimes colleges also ask for SAT II test results. **Starting to prepare for these tests early on is key.** By taking the exams in your junior year, you still have time during your senior fall to take them again and increase your score in order to obtain admission to your chosen school or to receive an academic scholarship.

At some schools, coaches have a lot of influence with Admissions and might be able to help to get you in, but at most schools they don't. Remember, admissions counselors ultimately **want to choose the type of student who will be successful and eventually graduate from their school.** Being on the low end of an academic profile and only being admitted for athletic reasons may not be in your best interest as a student-athlete. If the work load is too hard and you are struggling to keep your grades high enough, you may not be eligible to play and ultimately graduate.

Speak with your high school guidance counselor early and often to make sure that you are taking the right classes to help you get into your dream school. Work as hard in the classroom as you do at your sport…in the long run, your future will depend on it!

COLLEGE ADMISSIONS

Essential Tips for the Admissions Process

PREPARE FOR HIGH SCHOOL

Do well in 8h grade so you can get into Honors and Advanced Placement courses in 9th grade!

KEEP YOUR GRADES UP

Starting in 9th grade, **every grade you earn** will be on your official transcript. So work hard, take the right courses and get the highest grade that you can.

COMPILE YOUR TEAM

You will need many people on your side throughout this process- **parents, guidance counselors, teachers, coaches, recruiting coordinators, etc.** Know your team and share your college and life goals.

MAKE YOUR LIST OF SCHOOLS

Start early in the process with a **broad number of very different schools**. Reach schools, likely schools, safety schools. Schools you can play at and schools that you can't.

DO YOUR RESEARCH

Start researching and visiting schools to try to figure out exactly **what you are looking for in your college experience**. What's important to you? Big? Small? High academic? Recognizable name? Student/Teacher ratio? Playing time?

KEEP TRACK

Starting in freshmen year, **keep a record of your transcripts, test scores, extracurriculars, clubs, philanthropy, volunteer opportunities, etc.** so that when it's time to apply, you have everything in one place.

VISIT YOUR TOP SCHOOLS

If you are sincerely interested in a school, **make a visit and ask the questions** that you need answers to, see the campus and talk to professors and students.

NAIL THE INTERVIEW

For schools that encourage an interview to help with admission, **make sure that you are prepared and professional**. They want to get to know you as a person and a student to see if you will succeed at their institution. So be yourself!

READ DIRECTIONS & MEET DEADLINES

Read all of the instructions on your application and make sure that you **include everything they ask for at one time.** Forgetting to hand things in does not show the school that you will be able to handle the academic rigor of college! Make sure that you know each schools Admission process and deadlines and **apply on time!**

WHAT DOES THAT MEAN?

When going through the Admissions process, there will most likely be terms you are hearing for the first time and you have no idea what they mean. All schools have a slightly different admissions process to figure out what type of student will succeed at their particular institution. *Early Decision! Regular Decision! Early Action! Rolling Admission!* **WHAT ON EARTH ARE THEY TALKING ABOUT!?**

The easiest thing to do is to ask the coach, with whom you have most likely been in contact, what their college's admission process is and what timeline you need to follow. Some colleges have an application deadline in mid-January, after which, you are unable to apply to that school at all. Other colleges will accept applications most of the way through the summer.

Furthermore, the coach may have expectations of when they would like you to *commit and subsequently apply*. For the coach, the sooner they fill their class with the players they want, the better.

Here are some terms that you may hear during the admissions process:

GLOSSARY OF TERMS

COLLEGE ADMISSIONS PROCESS

▶ APPLICATION PROCESS

Advanced Placement (AP): A program in the United States and Canada created by the College Board which offers college-level curricula and examinations to high school students. American colleges and universities may grant placement and course credit to students who obtain high scores on the examinations.

Campus Interview: An in-person conversation with a faculty member, admissions officer, alumnus, or other institutional representative. Interviews are often not required but are a good idea in order to make a personal contact with a member of the campus community.

Campus Tour/Visit: A tour of a college or university's campus. Prospective students, their family members and other visitors take campus tours to learn about the college or university's facilities, as well as student life, culture on campus, academics, and programs offered by the institution.

College Essay: A brief composition, written on a specific subject, that is typically required by many colleges as part of the application process.

College Fair: A college fair is an event in which college admissions representatives come together at a school, community-gathering place or large convention center to meet face-to-face with high school students (and parents) to talk about their respective colleges and answer questions.

College Rep Visit: When a college or university representative visits a high school or community site to talk to prospective students about their institution. They also often conduct official off-campus interviews when visiting a site far from their institution.

Common Application (informally known as the Common App): Allows students to use one admissions application to apply to over 700 member colleges and universities. This allows the application to be filled out once and submitted to many schools that require the same information. Some schools may require supplemental information so be sure to check. There is a Common App for First-Year students and a Common App for Transfer students.

Core Courses: A series of high school courses required by the NCAA in order to compete at the Division I and Division II level. For an explanation and calculation of required core courses, visit the NCAA section of this book.

Demonstrated Interest: A student's expression of his or her desire to attend a particular institution through campus visits, campus interviews, contact with admissions and financial aid personnel. While not all institutions use this as a factor, a significant number of schools will consider demonstrated interest in their admissions decisions.

Extracurriculars: Any activities that you participate in that are not a high school course or paid employment. Can include school activities like yearbook, band, Spanish club or a sport, but also includes community activities like Boy Scouts, participating in a fundraiser or volunteering at the soup kitchen.

First-Generation Student: A student who is the first in their family to attend college.

Grade Point Average (GPA): A quantitative measure of a student's grades. It's important to maintain a high GPA starting during freshmen year to have the most opportunities to choose a good school.

COLLEGE ADMISSIONS DEFINITIONS

High School Profile: An overview of your high school that is submitted to the admissions office along with your official transcript. Information includes grading systems, course offerings and other features of the school. The admissions office uses this information to compare your GPA and courses to other applicants in your class.

Honors Classes: Classes that are similar to the regular class (English 1 vs. English 1 Honors) in the content that they offer except that they are enriched with studying the content in greater depth and at a faster pace.

In-state (Resident) Student: A student whose permanent residence is in the same state as the institution that he or she plans to attend. Tuition is often lower for in-state students. Be aware that most private institutions do not have in-state and out-of-state tuition costs.

Out-of-state (Non-resident) Student: A student whose permanent residence is not in the same state as the institution that he or she plans to attend. Out-of-state students often pay a higher tuition rate.

Placement Tests: Colleges use placement tests in subjects like math and English to check the academic skill levels of entering students. Then the college can place each student in classes at the right level.

Recommendations: Statements or letters of endorsement written on the student's behalf that are often used in the admissions process.

Selectivity: A selective college is a college that does not admit everyone. Selectivity is measured by the percentage of students who are admitted. Essentially, most colleges are selective to some degree. A small group of highly selective schools admits less than one third of those students who apply.

Transcript: A document that contains the record of a student's academic performance and test scores. An official, signed version of this document must be submitted, along with the application, directly from the high school where the prospective student attended.

Transfer Student: Any student applying to a college who has already attended another college.

▶ ENTRANCE EXAMS

ACT: A standardized examination that tests knowledge and achievement in four areas- English, math, reading and science reasoning. This exam is scored on a scale of 1-36 and is used to assess a student's readiness for college level instruction.

General Education Development Test (GED): A test taken by anyone 16 or older who has not graduated from, or is currently enrolled, in high school. It is made up of four tests that cover four different high school subjects. If one passes these tests, they will receive their high school equivalency diploma.

PLAN Test: An ACT preparation test usually taken in the sophomore year.

Preliminary scholastic Aptitude Test (PSAT): An SAT preparation test that is also used to qualify students for the National Merit Scholarship semifinals and other academic awards.

Scholastic Aptitude Test (SAT): A standardized examination that features three main sections: math, reading and writing. It also includes a written essay. Students may earn up to 2400 points (800 points in each section). Be sure to ask if your college accepts all three parts or just two.

SAT Subject Test (SAT II): Also known as SAT II, these tests are offered in many subjects including math, science, English, history and foreign languages. Some colleges may require one or more subject tests when applying for admission.

▶ ACCEPTANCE TERMS

Acceptance: When a college officially offers for you to enroll at their institution.

Articulation Agreement: Formal partnerships between at least two institutions of higher education. Typically, these agreements exist between a community college and a four-year institution, or a four-year institution and a graduate school. The goal is to create a seamless transfer for students from one institution to the next.

Deferred Admission: After applying Early Decision or Early Action to a school, your application may be held to be reviewed during a later application pool. You have not been denied admission at this point but they will now reconsider your application again during the Regular Decision process.

Deferred Enrollment: Available at some institutions for accepted students to postpone their enrollment to take a semester or a year off before starting school. You would typically have to have a very good reason to use deferred enrollment.

Denial: The decision through the admissions process to not offer a student admission to a particular college.

Early Action: A college admission policy that allows applicants to apply and receive notice of their admission, denial or deferment early. Applicants accepted under early action *are not under a binding agreement* to attend that school and may submit applications to other schools.

Early Admission: A program in which exceptional high school students with outstanding academic records may forgo their senior year and enroll in a college or university early.

Early Decision: A college admission policy that allows applicants, who commit to attend that school, to apply and receive notice of their admission, denial or deferment early. *A student may only apply Early Decision to one school. If the applicant is accepted, the student is obligated to attend that school and must withdraw all other applications.*

Regular Decision/Admission: An admissions process by which students apply by published deadlines, with promise of receiving an admissions decision no later than April 1 of their senior year.

Rolling Admission: An admissions process used by some institutions in which they will review and complete applications as they arrive, rather than by a set deadline. Students *are not under a binding agreement to attend if accepted during this process.*

Waitlist: If an applicant is placed on the waitlist, they will only be offered the opportunity to enroll in the institution if there is space available after all fully admitted students have responded to their admission offer.

▶ POST-ACCEPTANCE TERMS

Audit: To attend a class without receiving credit for the class.

Credit Hour: Credit given for attending one lecture hour of class each week. Most college classes are three credit hours, meaning their total meeting time per week is three hours.

Developmental education: Instructional and support activities designed to keep unprepared students in college and help them improve their basic skills so that they can successfully complete a program and achieve their educational goals.

Enrollment: Attending a school and being enrolled in classes.

Matriculation: The payment of deposits, tuition, fees, and all other charges to enroll at an educational institution.

Major: A student's concentrated field of study.

Minor: A student's secondary field of study.

Placement Tests: Tests that measure the academic skills needed for college-level work. They cover reading, math, and other subjects. Placement test results help determine what courses a student is ready for and whether they would benefit from remedial classes.

Prerequisite: A course that must be taken prior to enrollment in another course.

Graduate Degrees: Degrees acquired after earning a bachelor's degree. Common graduate degrees include a master's degree (MA), doctoral degree (PhD), master's of business administration (MBA), and medical doctor (MD).

Certificates: College certificate programs offer you an alternative academic credential to the lengthier undergraduate or graduate degree programs. The coursework of such programs tends to be compressed, focusing almost entirely on a specific topic.

▶ TYPES OF POST-SECONDARY INSTITUTIONS

College: A wide range of higher educational institutions including those that offer two- to four-year programs in the arts and sciences.

Community College: Also known as junior colleges, technical colleges or city colleges. Primarily a two-year school providing higher education as well as lower-level courses, granting certificates, diplomas and associate's degrees. Many also offer continuing and adult education.

Graduate School: An institution that offers degree programs beyond a bachelor's degree.

Liberal Arts College: An institution there the academic focus is on developing the intellect and instruction in the humanities and sciences, rather than on training for a particular vocational, technical of professional pursuit.

Private Institution: And independent school that sets its own policies and goals and is privately funded. These are typically smaller schools with an average of about 2000 students. Private schools do not receive government funds.

Proprietary Institution: Refers to higher educational institutions that are operated by private, profit seeking businesses.

Public Institution: A college or university that is predominantly funded by public means through the government.

University: An institution that provides graduate and professional education in addition to a four-year post-secondary education.

Vocational or Technical School: An institution that provides post-secondary education and job or skill training. These schools typically offer shorter, career-specific training without many unrelated course requirements.

Religion-based institution: A college or university established under the sponsorship of a church, synagogue, or mosque: a denomination: or a particular religion. Most religion-based schools accept students of other faiths. There is often a religious aspect required in the curriculum.

▶ TYPES OF POST-SECONDARY DEGREES

A.A.: Associate of Arts- can be earned at most two-year colleges.

A.A.S.: Associate of Applied Science- can be earned at some two-year colleges.

B.A.: Bachelor of Arts—can be earned at four-year colleges.

B.S.: Bachelor of Science—can be earned at four-year colleges

My Notes About College Admissions:

UNDERSTANDING
Financial Aid

OK...let's be honest...

FOR MOST FAMILIES, THIS IS THE MOST STRESSFUL PART OF THE COLLEGE DECISION-MAKING PROCESS.

The cost of college can range from **$10,000** to over **$60,000** per year! Trying to figure out how your family will pay for college is certainly an important step in the process.

FINDING THE RIGHT PRICE CAN BE A BIG CHALLENGE.

Of course, most athletes are hoping that a Division 1 coach is going to walk up to them one day and offer them a full ride to the greatest college on the planet, at which they will eventually win a National Championship and be an All-American MVP and go on to play professionally and make millions of dollars on car commercials alone.

REALITY CHECK...that will only happen to an extremely low percentage of all high school athletes. The rest of us will have to settle for having an amazing college experience, making lifelong friends with our teammates while earning a degree that will eventually land us a great job where we will earn the millions of dollars through hard work. *(OK...probably not millions but maybe just aim for a good, healthy living).*

Most families are looking for the best marriage between the academic and athletic experience along with making sure they can afford to pay for it. As an athlete, you aren't necessarily paying attention to the affordability of a school, but more likely the one that fits your academic and athletic goals. You, as the one in need of the college education, must sit down with your parents and have an **open and honest conversation about their expectations when it comes to paying for college.**

Are they able to pay fully and money isn't an issue? Are you on your own to pay for school? Will they pay up to a certain amount and you are responsible for the rest of it if you choose a more expensive school? If so, are you willing to come out with debt? How much debt is acceptable to you? All of these questions will help guide you towards a list of schools that are attainable for you financially, and may also help you to cross a few schools off your list.

Don't necessarily count out expensive colleges immediately if a coach contacts you—they will often meet a family's need as long as you meet their academic profile. Often, you can check their website to see the average cost for a typical student after scholarships and grants. Filling out the FAFSA form is a good start to help you know what your family's expected contribution will be.

Finally, almost every school packages financial aid differently. Some will combine academic and athletic scholarships. Others will take the higher of the two. Some schools will package solely based on need, while others will give high academic scholarships to the students who fit their profile, regardless of need.

Be sure to speak with the coach if you have concerns about the cost of a school.

Essential Tips for the Financial Aid Process

KNOW YOUR EFC
Be sure to figure out your Expected Family Contribution (EFC). This will tell you how much your family can expect to pay for college per year. Go to collegeboard.com or finaid.org to get an idea of your EFC.

USE THE NET PRICE CALCULATOR
Fill out the college's net price calculator online if you are interested in attending their school. You can often fill in what scholarship you might qualify for and as long as all of you other information is correct, you will get a price that is typically within a few thousand dollars of your financial aid package presented later on.

WHAT'S IN A NAME?
When receiving your financial aid package, don't get hung up on how much you received in an "athletic" scholarship vs. an "academic" scholarship vs. "need-based" aid. A discount is a discount!

EARLY MAY BE BETTER
If you have researched schools and found a good fit that you are comfortable with, think about applying early (Early Decision, etc.). There is more scholarship and grant money available early and for those who are definitely planning on attending the school. Later in the process, money is spread out among those who "might" attend.

DON'T GIVE IN TO STICKER SHOCK
Try not to be afraid of the high cost of an institution. If you meet their academic profile and are accepted, they will often meet your EFC and make up the difference in grants and scholarships.

GIVE THEM A CALL!
After filling out the Net Price Calculator, feel free to call the Financial Aid office to make sure that you did not miss anything. They can help you through the process and answer any questions you may have. Although they cannot tell you what scholarship you will receive, if any, because they do not make those decisions!

FILL IT OUT REGARDLESS
Fill out the FAFSA even if you don't think that you qualify for need-based aid—the criteria changes every year so you don't want to leave money on the table if you don't have to!

BARGAIN HUNT!
Be sure to check for any local or corporate scholarships that might be available. Even if you don't qualify for need-based aid through the FAFSA, you can still acquire private awards and scholarships that will save you money.

PAY ATTENTION TO DEADLINES
Make sure that you are paying attention to when your financial paperwork is due. The earlier the better so you don't miss out.

ASK!!
If you feel like you might qualify for a higher scholarship or may need a little bit more grant money, ASK! The worst they can say is no, but often, if you have a good reason, they can make an adjustment. You never know if you don't ask!

WHAT DOES THAT MEAN?

The Financial Aid process, although overwhelming, is a necessary part of finding the right college for you. Those who can **tackle it head-on and are not afraid to ask questions** will be able to navigate the waters a little bit easier. When you are meeting with coaches and financial aid counselors, it will be important to have a general understanding of the terms that they are using.

How do you know how to fill out an NPC to get your EFC to find out the CoA? When can you fill out the FAFSA and figure out if you need a loan, a grant or a scholarship? Do I have to pay all of that back or not???

The following terms are an overview of what you can expect to hear from coaches and counselors throughout the financial aid process.

GLOSSARY OF TERMS

THE FINANCIAL AID PROCESS

▶ **BASIC TERMS**

Award Letter: When a college officially informs you of how much aid you will get in scholarships and grants.

Cost of Attendance (CoA): The total amount it will cost you to go to school—usually stated as a yearly figure. CoA includes tuition and fees; room and board (or a housing and food allowance); and allowances for books, supplies, transportation, loan fees, and dependent care. It also includes miscellaneous and personal expenses, including an allowance for the rental or purchase of a personal computer; costs related to a disability; and reasonable costs for eligible study-abroad programs. Contact the financial aid administrator at the school you're planning to attend if you have any unusual expenses that might affect your CoA.

Demonstrated Financial Need: The difference between your Expected Family Contribution (EFC) and the Cost of Attendance (CoA) at a particular school. For example, if the CoA is $45,000 and your EFC is $20,000, then your demonstrated financial need is $25,000. While CoA varies from school to school, your EFC does not change based on the school you attend.

Expected Family Contribution (EFC): The total amount that a family will be expected to pay to attend college. This is determined based on a family's income and assets.

FAFSA: The Free Application for Federal Student Aid. You must complete the FAFSA form annually in order to apply for federal student aid such as federal student grants, work-study and loans. Many colleges use the FAFSA to determine your financial need in order to decide whether or not you qualify for their aid. The FAFSA is available to be filled out in October of your senior year.

Fees: Charges that cover the costs not associated with a student's course load such as clubs, Greek life, athletic events, etc.

Financial Aid Package: The total amount of financial aid (federal and non-federal) a student is offered by a college or career school. The school's financial aid staff combines various forms of aid into a "package" to help meet a student's education costs.

Need-Blind Admission: A policy of making admissions decisions without regard to the student's need for financial aid.

Net Price: An estimate of the actual cost per year that a student and their family will need to pay to cover the cost of education expenses. This is determined by subtracting a student's grants and scholarships from the cost of attendance.

Net Price Calculator (NPC): An online tool provided by each college to estimate the net price a family can expect to pay to attend their institution.

Tuition: The amount of money charged by a college for classroom and other instruction. Basically, the cost of taking classes at that institution. This does not include things like room and board or textbooks.

▶ SCHOLARSHIPS

Academic: Money given based upon a student's academic achievement as reflected in your college application.

Athletic: Money given based upon athletic ability.

Corporate: Money awarded by corporations to help employees and their families, show community support, or to encourage future job seekers toward a career in the company's area of business.

Private Organization: These scholarships are readily available from many organizations. Some examples of these organizations are school districts, places of worship, chambers of commerce and labor unions.

▶ LOANS

Loans can be attained through many different venues and typically must be repaid.

Federal Student Loan: A loan funded by the federal government to help pay for your education. A federal student loan is borrowed money you must repay with interest.

Federal Perkins Loans: The Federal Perkins Loan Program provides money for college or career school for students with financial need. Check with your school's financial aid office to see if your school participates in the Federal Perkins Loan Program. Loans made through the Federal Perkins Loan Program, often called Perkins Loans, are low-interest federal student loans for undergraduate and graduate students with exceptional financial need. Visit their website at **www.studentaid.ed.gov.**

Institutional Loan: A loan given to a student through the college or university itself.

Direct PLUS (Parent Loans for Undergraduate Students) Loan: PLUS loans are federal loans that graduate or professional students and parents of dependent undergraduate students can use to help pay for college or career school. PLUS loans can help pay for education expenses not covered by other financial aid. The U.S. Department of Education makes Direct PLUS Loans to eligible borrowers through schools participating in the Direct Loan Program. Visit their website at **www.studentaid.ed.gov.**

Stafford Loan: A student loan administered by the college or university using the institution's funds as the source of funding. Perkins Loans may be considered institutional loans.

Subsidized and Unsubsidized Loans: The U.S. Department of Education offers low-interest loans to eligible students to help cover the cost of college or career school. Students may be eligible to receive subsidized and unsubsidized loans based on their financial need. Subsidized and unsubsidized loans are federal student loans for eligible students to help cover the cost of higher education at a four-year college or university, community college, or trade, career, or technical school. The U.S. Department of Education offers eligible students at participating schools Direct Subsidized Loans and Direct Unsubsidized Loans. Visit their website at **studentaid.ed.gov.**

Unsubsidized Loans: Can qualify regardless of financial need or income. This loan accrues interest throughout the life of the loan. This type of loan is available to undergraduate or graduate students.

Subsidized Loans: Based on financial need. This loan does not accrue interest while the student is in college because the interest is paid by the government. This type of loan is only available to undergraduate students.

William Ford Direct Loan Program: A federal student loan, made through the William D. Ford Federal Direct Loan Program that allows eligible students and parents to borrow directly from the U.S. Department of Education at participating schools.

▶ GRANTS

Grants can be attained through many different venues and most often do not need to be repaid. Check the fine print and be sure to ask the originator of the grant.

Federal Pell Grant: Federal Pell Grants are usually awarded only to undergraduate students. The amount of aid you can receive depends on your financial need, the cost of attendance at your school, and more. Federal Pell Grants usually are awarded only to undergraduate students who have not earned a bachelor's or a professional degree. (In some cases, however, a student enrolled in a *post-baccalaureate teacher certification program* might receive a *Federal Pell Grant*.) A Federal Pell Grant, unlike a loan, does not have to be repaid, except under certain circumstances.

Federal Supplemental Educational Opportunity (FSEOG) Grant: Grant- The FSEOG program is administered directly by the financial aid office at each participating school. Not all schools participate. Check with your school's financial aid office to find out if the school offers the FSEOG.

Teacher Education Assistance for College and Higher Education (TEACH) Grant: A TEACH Grant is different from other federal student grants because it requires you to take certain kinds of classes in order to get the grant, and then do a certain kind of job to keep the grant from turning into a loan. A TEACH Grant can help you pay for college if you plan to become a teacher in a high-need field in a low-income area. *You'll be required to teach for a certain length of time, so make sure you understand your obligation.*

Aid for military families: You may be able to get money for college or career school for your or your family member's military service. Scholarships and loan repayment assistance are available from a number of sources. Both the federal government and nonprofit organizations offer money for college to veterans, future military personnel, active duty personnel, or those related to veterans or active duty personnel.

Institutional Grant: A need-based grant provided by an institution and offered to those students whose families are unable to pay for their education. Institutional grants do not have to be repaid.

Merit-based Grant: A form of gift aid, or scholarship, based upon your GPA, academic achievement and extracurricular involvement with some attention to your financial need. Merit-based grants do not need to be repaid.

Need-based Grant: A grant offered as part of a financial aid package when a student or their family is unable to pay the full cost of attending an institution. Often based on your FAFSA results. This grant does not need to be repaid.

▶ WORK-STUDY PROGRAMS

Most colleges offer work-study programs that allow students to work part-time while attending classes to help supplement their financial aid package. They most often work a job on-campus and the money that they earn is used to help pay their tuition.

My Notes About Financial Aid:

WHAT'S THE *difference* BETWEEN

COLLEGIATE ATHLETIC ASSOCIATIONS

NCAA DIVISION I— *Prestige & Size*

Competing at the DI level is almost every athlete's original dream. **Big events, big crowds, and big competition.** Realize with all of that glory, you can often get overwhelmed by the amount of time your sport will take from you. You will not have free time because your time is not yours. Between practice, travel, competitions, study halls, weight training, volunteering, etc. you will not be in charge of your schedule and what you can participate in outside of your sport. However, that could also be exactly what you are looking for and can be an amazing experience for the right student-athlete.

NCAA DIVISION II— *Balanced Opportunities*

Not all athletes dream of the pressure that comes with Division I athletics but they still want a **high level of competition in a smaller atmosphere.** Some exceptional student-athletes may prefer the opportunity to play all four years instead of waiting and hoping for their shot in their junior or senior year. DII is also a great chance for those who may have struggled a bit academically in high school because the requirements for eligibility are slightly lower. Division II also offers a more balanced college life than you could get at the DI level.

NCAA DIVISION III— *Well-Rounded & Underrated*

Surprisingly enough, even though Division III does not offer athletic scholarships, about 80% of student-athletes receive some sort of non-athletic aid to attend their school. Which is much higher than the 55% of scholarships to DI and 60% to DII. DIII programs offer **a well-rounded college experience** in which playing seasons are more limited and give students the opportunity to participate in other things on and off campus like clubs, immersion trips and internships. DIII sports are still highly competitive, contrary to popular belief because of the structure of the divisions.

NJCAA— *A Running Start*

If you are looking to save some money or maybe stay close to home and **get a jumpstart on your college degree,** a junior college in the NJCAA could be a great place to start. Junior colleges can also be a good dip into the rigor of college like for students who struggled academically in high school. Athletically, it often leads to playing all four years of college - two years at your junior college and then when you transfer to a four-year school, you already have two years of experience and growth in your sport under your belt so you can often have a leg up to a starting spot.

NAIA— *Opportunity & Community*

Many consider the time commitment and competition level of NAIA to be on par with NCAA Division II or III. However, they have the **ability to offer athletic scholarships**. The NAIA gives out over $500 million in athletic scholarships every year. So if you are looking for a **community feeling and the ability to do a lot on campus** but also need monetary aid, NAIA could be right for you.

NCAA

THE NATIONAL COLLEGIATE ATHLETIC ASSOCIATION contains more than 1,100 colleges and universities with almost 500,000 athletes on 19,500 teams. NCAA member schools include colleges with less than 1,000 students and universities that have tens of thousands.

The NCAA consists of three divisions in which they place colleges with similar size and structure **to create an even playing field amongst the teams and provide more opportunities for athletes to compete in National Championships.** Division I schools typically consist of large universities and colleges and tend to have the largest athletic budgets and offer the highest number of athletic scholarships. Division II schools are typically smaller than DI schools, have fewer financial resources and can only offer partial scholarships to athletes. Division III institutions are the smallest schools in the NCAA and are not allowed to offer athletic scholarships.

▶ Academic Requirements

Each NCAA division has different academic requirements to follow. Division I and II require a certification from the NCAA Eligibility Center that states that your core course requirements and progression regulations have been followed all four years of high school. You must then also meet the sometimes more stringent requirements for admission to the school. For Division III you must simply be able to be accepted based on the institution's academic requirements for admission.

Please refer to the NCAA-specific section of this book for a closer look at the academic requirements of the NCAA.

▶ Athletic Eligibility

Student-athletes at the Division I level will have five calendar years to participate in four seasons of competition. Division II and III student-athletes may also only compete in four seasons of competition but will operate under the first 10-semester or 15-quarter rule. (See Recruiting Definitions for an explanation.) Every student-athlete must also be making progress toward a degree in any field and carry a minimum number of credits per semester in order to remain eligible.

All NCAA student-athletes must also maintain amateur status throughout their entire college career in order to be eligible to play.

You can rely on your coach and compliance officers to help you make your schedule in a way that keeps you eligible to play while in college.

Scholarships

Division I and II schools provide more than **$2.5 billion in athletic scholarships** every year to more than 150,000 student-athletes. Although Division III schools do not provide athletic scholarships, the vast majority of DIII student-athletes are eligible for, and receive, academic scholarships and need-based aid.

It is important to realize that only about 2% of high school athletes will receive an athletic scholarship within the NCAA and only a fraction of those students become professional athletes. Student-athletes should keep this in mind when they are talking to coaches from different schools and different divisions. Your education is the most important part of going to college! Often, you will receive more scholarship money in merit-based aid for having good grades than you will receive from an athletic scholarship.

The NCAA dictates how many scholarships each sport can offer in Divisions I and II. To get the most benefit from these limits, coaches will often split them into smaller scholarships in order to offer money to many athletes on their team.

One thing to know is that even though the NCAA puts a maximum on the number of scholarships each sport can offer, **the school itself may not have that many scholarships available to give away.** For instance, Division I Women's Volleyball can offer a total of 12 scholarships. However, there are many schools who will only give funding for 9, or 6, or 4.5 scholarships total based on the money that is available to them. So the smaller DI schools tend to have way fewer scholarships to hand out altogether.

Recruiting Rules

Recruiting rules in the NCAA are the most strict of all of the athletic associations. Divisions I and II have many different rules about how and when they can contact prospective student-athletes, while Division III is less restrictive. Because all of the contact rules are so different, please see the "Deeper Dive Into the NCAA" section to learn more about the rules within each division.

See the"Deeper Dive into the NCAA" section for more specific information regarding the different Divisions within the NCAA.

NCAA

NJCAA

THE NATIONAL JUNIOR COLLEGE ATHLETIC ASSOCIATION, often also referred to as JuCo, is made up of two-year and junior colleges and many of its members are community colleges. There are more than 525 member institutions and it is similar to the NCAA in that is it divided into three divisions. Division I can offer full scholarships and Division II can offer scholarships limited to tuition, fees and books. Division III may not provide any athletically-related scholarships.

NJCAA schools can be a good option if student-athletes do not have grades that qualify for some of the 4-year schools they are interested in. They can often spend the first two years at a school where they can improve their grades while also playing their sport. The student-athlete will often earn their Associates Degree and get a lot of their general education requirements completed so they can focus on their major when transferring to a four-year school.

▶ Academic Requirements

To obtain eligibility in the NJCAA, a student-athlete must either graduate from an accredited high school or obtain a General Education Diploma (GED).

Non-high school graduates may still obtain athletic eligibility by completing one term of college work and pass 12 credits with at least a 1.75 GPA.

▶ Athletic Eligibility

Student-athletes participating in any one of the certified sports of the NJCAA must conform to the

requirements of the NJCAA Rules of Eligibility, the rules and regulations of the conference and region with which the college is affiliated, and also the rules of the college at which the students are attending and participating.

A student-athlete is allowed two seasons of competition in any sport if they did not participate in two seasons previously. There is also no clock or age limit at the NJCAA level. You still have eligibility if you have not previously competed in your first two or more years of intercollegiate competition in that sport.

Similarly to the NCAA, the NJCAA does have a Letter of Intent that commits a student-athlete for a period of one academic year.

► Scholarships

The NJCAA offers scholarships in a similar manner to the NCAA in which a certain number of scholarships are awarded per team. All NJCAA sports are head-count sports. This means each sport has an absolute number of scholarships that it can award and the amount of athletes receiving scholarships on that team cannot exceed that amount.

For example, women's lacrosse can award up to 20 athletic scholarships. Although each school can allot less scholarships if they choose, there may not be more than 20 athletes on the lacrosse team receiving athletic aid at any given time.

Scholarship Limits Per Sport

Men's Sports		Women's Sports	
Baseball	24	Basketball	15
Basketball	15	Beach Volleyball	10
Bowling	12	Bowling	12
Cross Country	10	Cross Country	10
Football	85	Golf	8
Golf	8	Lacrosse	20
Ice Hockey	16	Soccer	24
Lacrosse	20	Softball	24
Soccer	24	Swimming/Diving	15
Swimming/Diving	15	Tennis	9
Tennis	9	Track & Field	20
Track & Field	20	Volleyball	14
Wrestling	20		

► Recruiting Rules

There are more than 500 junior colleges and each is part of one of 24 regions throughout the country. Each region has the ability to make their own set of rules and standards above and beyond (but never below) the very basic rules set forth by the NJCAA.

As far as contact is concerned, there are no specific contact rules so coaches may speak to players of any age at any time.

Due to the unique academic and athletic situation of each individual, and the complexity of the NJCAA eligibility rules, it is recommended that each potential student-athlete discuss their athletic eligibility with the coach at the NJCAA college where they are being recruited or are choosing to attend.

NAIA

THE NATIONAL ASSOCIATION FOR INTERCOLLEGIATE ATHLETICS is the oldest college athletics governing body. It consists of over 200 mostly smaller, private schools and was started to offer sports organization for smaller and less wealthy schools. Currently, the NAIA has 25 sports that include 60,000 athletes and gives over $600 million in scholarships.

Admissions requirements are similar to NCAA Division III where a student-athlete must simply meet the same admissions standards and requirements of the general student body.

The appeal of an NAIA school is that, also similar to NCAA DIII, there are smaller campuses and smaller class sizes. With fewer restrictions on recruiting, you also have a good opportunity to get to know the coach, the school and their athletic program better before you make a choice.

▶ Academic Requirements

To obtain eligibility in the NAIA, a student-athlete must meet the following:

A. Graduate from an accredited high school.

B. Meet 2 of the 3 following criteria:
- **Test scores**—minimum of 16 on the ACT or 860 on the SAT
- **GPA**—Minimum overall GPA of 2.0 on a 4.0 scale
- **Class Rank**—Graduate in the top half of the class

Refer to NAIA.org for requirements for home-schooled, international or GED students.

▶ Athletic Eligibility

Each athlete has 10 semesters to play four seasons in the NAIA. To remain eligible, you must take at least 12 credit hours at all times and be progressing toward a degree. Once starting your junior year, you must maintain at least a 2.0 GPA, which will be evaluated at the end of each semester.

▶ Scholarships

Scholarships and aid are also similar to DI and DII schools in that each sport has a limit on the total amount of financial aid given as full or partial scholarships to student-athletes.

- Scholarships can be given as full, half or quarter awards to as many student-athletes as the coach decides. But these scholarships cannot exceed to total number specified for that sport.
- Academically gifted students can be exempted from these limits if they meet grade or test score criteria established by the NAIA.

Aid to the student-athlete must be limited to the actual cost of:
- Tuition
- Mandatory fees, books and supplies required for the student's courses
- Room and board based on board allowance in college catalog

NAIA

Aid to the student-athlete must be limited to the actual cost of:

- Tuition
- Mandatory fees, books and supplies required for the student's courses
- Room and board based on board allowance in college catalog

Scholarship Limits Per Sport

Men's Sports

Baseball	12
Basketball (Div I)	11
Basketball (Div II)	6
Cross Country	5
Football	24
Golf	5
Soccer	12
Swimming/Diving	8
Tennis	5
Track & Field	12
Wrestling	8

Women's Sports

Basketball (Div I)	11
Basketball (Div II)	6
Cross Country	5
Golf	5
Soccer	12
Softball	10
Swimming/Diving	8
Tennis	5
Track & Field	12
Volleyball	8

▶ Recruiting Rules

Recruiting rules are much less strict than NCAA. The NAIA does not regulate the amount of contact or

the time of year that a coach can contact a prospective student-athlete. So a coach can contact you at any age at any time. It is their belief that more contact can create a better relationship between the coach and player to help you make a better, more informed decision.

You may participate in up to two tryouts on the college's campus but they cannot interfere with your time in school.

NAIA

▶ NAIA ELIGIBILITY CENTER

Students must receive an eligible decision by the NAIA Eligibility Center to compete within the NAIA. All Student-athletes interested in playing at an NAIA college for the first time must register online. This includes high school seniors and transfers from two- and four-year colleges.

To register with the NAIA, go to PLAYNAIA.ORG

You will need:

- Current contact info
- Previous residences and addresses
- High schools attended
- Sports participation history

→ Be sure to include the NAIA Eligibility Center Code (9876) to have your standardized test scores sent there.

→ Have your high school counselor send the NAIA Eligibility Center a final, official transcript.

→ There is a registration fee — refer to the website for cost and opportunities to have it waived if you meet certain criteria.

WHAT DOES THAT MEAN?

When going through the recruiting process, **there are so many rules that coaches need to abide by** that it sometimes seems daunting to follow them all, and each of the associations have their own set of rules. What is a dead period? A quiet period? An evaluation period? Why are they necessary? Do all coaches from every sport have the same rules?

The answers to these questions can be confusing and hard to keep up with when you are a student-athlete trying to find your ideal college. **Can you call a coach? When can they call you? Can you talk to them when they come watch you play?** Unfortunately, there is no one answer to all of these questions and the countless others. Division I is slightly different than Division II which is way different from Division III. NAIA is even less restrictive then all NCAA divisions (see the NAIA section for more info on that).

The following definitions are a compilation of many NCAA terms and what they mean, as well as a recruiting chart to demonstrate the difference between the divisions:

GLOSSARY OF TERMS

RECRUITING DEFINITIONS

▶ **RECRUITING DEFINITIONS**

Academic Redshirt: When an athlete is required to sit out their freshmen year because they did not meet certain academic requirements in high school.

Amateur Status: All NCAA student-athletes must be considered amateurs in order to compete in any sport. To maintain your amateur status, you must not have a written or verbal agreement with an agent, receive money beyond actual and necessary expenses, play or tryout for a professional team, or delay your college enrollment to participate in competitions.

Celebratory Signing Form: A standardized, non-binding form provided by the NCAA to a college-bound student-athlete who is attending a Division III institution. This form is provided to those attending Division III institutions in order to mimic the National Letter of Intent signed by Division I and II student-athletes but is only intended as a celebration of their commitment and cannot be considered binding.

Off-campus Contact: Any time a college coach has a conversation beyond a simple "hello" with you or your parents outside the college campus.

Core Courses: College-bound student-athletes must take a specific set of NCAA-approved courses throughout their four years of high school in order to qualify for to play at the Division I or Division II level.

Equivalency Sports: A term referring to how scholarships can be offered in DI and DII. Equivalency sports are allowed to take their maximum amount of allowable scholarships and split them amongst as many players as the coach decides. Example: DI Men's soccer is allowed 9.9 scholarships and the coach can divide that up among 20 athletes if they would like.

Evaluation: When a college coach watches you compete or practice.

Head Count Sports: A term referring to how scholarships can be offered in NCAA DI and DII. Head count sports scholarships are absolute and the number of athletes receiving a scholarship must not exceed that number. Example: DI Women's Basketball may not have more than 15 players on the team receiving athletic aid. Fully funded teams often Give their student-athletes full scholarships.

Institutional request list (IRL): When an NCAA Division I and/or II school is interested in recruiting a student-athlete, they will add the college bound student-athlete to the IRL to inform the NCAA Eligibility Center of the institution's interest in having an academic certification decision for the student-athlete.

National Letter of Intent (NLI): A binding aggreement between a student-athlete and a NLI member institution that states that the student-athlete agrees to attend the institution on a full-time basis for one academic year in exchange for one year of athletically-related financial aid.

Official Commitment: When you sign a National Letter of Intent, you have officially committed to attend that institution for one academic year.

Official Visit: On an official NCAA visit, the college can pay for multiple expenses for you and your parents or guardians. This expense and amount can include meals, transportation and reasonable entertainment expenses but amounts can vary by division. Requirements before your visit, such as transcripts and test scores, also varies by division and is something the college coach will know and ask for. You may only take a specific total amount of official visits for DI and DII schools.

Recruiting Calendar: NCAA member schools limit recruiting to certain periods during the year. Recruiting calendars promote the well-being of college-bound student-athletes and ensure fairness among schools by defining certain periods during the year in which recruiting may or may not occur in a particular sport. ***Division III schools do not have a specific recruiting calendar and may contact you or your parents at any time of year.***

> **Contact Period:** A timeframe in which a college coach may have face-to-face contact with you or your parents, may write to you or your parents, may watch you play, or visit your high school.

RECRUITING DEFINITIONS

Dead Period: A timeframe in which a college coach may not have face-to-face contact with you or your parents on or off campus, and may not watch you compete or visit your high school. They may, however, write to or call you during this time.

Evaluation Period: A timeframe in which a college coach may watch you compete or practice, visit your high school, or write to or call you or your parents. However, a coach may not have face-to-face contact with you or your parents off of the college's campus.

Quiet Period: A timeframe in which a college coach may not have any in-person contact with you or your parents off the college's campus .The coach may not watch you play or visit your high school during this time. You may visit a college campus during this time and a coach may write or call.

Redshirt: An athlete can take one season to "redshirt" for academic or injury reasons. In this season, the athlete can still be on scholarship and participate in practice but they may not compete. When you redshirt for any reason, you will not use a season of eligibility and will still have that season left to compete.

Unofficial Visit: Any visit to a college campus by you or your parents where you pay your own expenses. The college my not pay for food or transportation but DI and DII may provide certain amounts of tickets to a home athletic contest. You may make an unlimited amount of unofficial visits at any time except in the sports of lacrosse, wrestling and women's gymnastics at the DI and DII levels. **Be aware, you may not talk with a coach during an unofficial visit during a dead period.**

Verbal Commitment: When you verbally agree to play sports for a college before signing a National Letter of Intent. Verbal commitments are not binding and can be made at any time in the recruiting process.

Walk-on: Someone who is not recruited by a school, but later joins part of the team by trying out. Walk-ons don't often receive scholarships their first year, but can earn one sometime throughout their career.

▶ YEARS OF ELIGIBILITY

Season of Competition: A student-athlete uses a season of competition the moment they step onto the court, field, gym or track during a collegiate competition, regardless of how long you play.

Five-year Clock: If you play at a Division I school, you have five calendar years in which to play four seasons of competition. Your five-year clock starts when you enroll as a full-time student at any college. Your clock continues even if you spend an academic year in residence as a result of transferring, decide to redshirt, do not attend school or attend school part time.

Ten-semester/ 15-quarter clock: If you play at a Division II or III school, you have the first 10 semesters or 15 quarters in which you are enrolled as a full-time student to complete your four seasons of participation. You use a semester or quarter any time you attend class as a full-time student or are enrolled part time and compete for the school. You do not use a term if you only attend part time with no competition or are not enrolled for a term.

My Notes:

Diving into the NCAA

The largest of the three Collegiate Athletic Associations is the NCAA. And while the NJCAA and the NAIA have different divisions within them, they are rather similar in structure and rules. The NCAA, however, has three divisions - all with very different rules to follow and requirements to meet.

Here, we will take a deeper look into the rules and requirements of each NCAA division starting with an explanation of the NCAA core courses, Eligibility Center and academic requirements.

NCAA CORE COURSES

The NCAA requires that all student-athletes take a series of classes in order to prepare them for the academic rigor of college. These core courses consist of NCAA-approved high school classes. In order to be considered an NCAA core course, it must meet these conditions:

1. **Be an academic, four-year college prep course in the following subjects:**
   - English
   - Math
   - Natural or Physical Science
   - Foreign Language
   - Comparative Religion or Philosophy

2. **Be taught at or above your high school's regular academic level.**

3. **Receive credit towards high school graduation and appear on an official transcript with course title, grade and credit awarded.**

Be aware that not all courses are created equal and many you will take will not count as NCAA core courses. This includes courses in these areas:

   A. Fine arts or vocations like art, band or orchestra, physical education, typing or shop class
   B. Prep courses for working in the world such as personal finance or tech prep
   C. Any courses taught below grade level or at a slower pace including fundamental, basic or foundational courses
   D. Non-academic courses like photography, cooking or greenhouse management
   E. Credit-by-exam courses

Always be sure to talk to your guidance counselor to receive a list of NCAA-approved core courses and use this workbook to make sure that you stay on track throughout your high school career.

The NCAA provides you with printable worksheets that will help you to calculate and keep track of your core course grades, credits, and quality points throughout school. You can find those worksheets at **NCAA.ORG**. Be sure to check your transcripts at the end of each year to make sure you have the correct grades and credits.

NCAA

CALCULATING YOUR CORE COURSE GPA

The NCAA Eligibility Center uses only the grades from your NCAA core courses to calculate your eligible GPA. They will take your best grades from the required number of course, so if you take more than the minimum, you can drop your lowest grades if they lower your GPA. Conversely, if the grades in those extra courses will improve your GPA, they will indeed count those grades too.

According to NCAA.org, here is how your transcripts will be interpreted and converted:

- **GPA is calculated on a 4.000 scale**
- **Numeric grades such as 93 or 87 are converted to letter grades**
- **Plus and minus are not used to calculate GPA- only letters**
- **Weighted honors and advanced placement courses can improve GPA only if your high school notifies the NCAA Eligibility Center that it weighs grades in those classes**
- **Pass/Fail classes will be assigned lowest possible passing grade of a D**

To figure out your eligibility status, your grades are then converted into **Quality Points** for each course. Then your Quality Points will be divided by the number of credits earned and that will give your core course GPA.

Quality Points	**Units of Credit (length class is taken)**
A= 4 points	**1 Quarter** = 0.25 units
B= 3 points	**1 Trimester** = 0.34 units
C= 2 points	**1 Semester** = 0.50 units
D= 1 point	**1 Year** = 1.0 units

Here is an example of how to calculate your **Quality Points:**

- If you receive a B (3 points) for a trimester course (0.34 units): *3 pts. x 0.34 units = 1.02*
- If you receive a B (3 points) for a semester course (0.50 units): *3 pts. x 0.50 units = 1.50*
- If you receive a B (3 points) for a full year course (1.00 units): *3 pts. x 1.00 units = 3*

NCAA

NCAA ELIGIBILITY CENTER

Division I and Division II require certification on the NCAA Eligibility Center (formerly known as the NCAA Clearinghouse). A student-athlete cannot sign a National Letter of Intent as an NCAA athlete in DI or DII without this certification. Division III does not require certification from the Eligibility Center but athletes can still create a free Profile Page and convert it to a Certification Account if necessary.

▶ *To register with the NCAA, go to* **ELIGIBILITYCENTER.ORG**

Choose from two account types to start:

- **Certification Account**—Needed in order to be recruited by or compete at a DI or DII school. Cannot go on official visits or sign and NLI without certification. There is a fee associated with creating this account.

- **Profile Page**—If you plan to compete at a DIII school or are not currently sure, you can start with a profile page. You can transition to a Certification Account at any point if necessary. Note: it is not a requirement to have a Profile Page in order to be recruited, commit to, or compete at a DIII school. The profile page is free.

▶ *Information needed to register:*

- Valid student email
- Basic student information
- Basic student education history
- Student sports participation history
- Payment if getting certification account-

**see website for information on if you qualify for a fee waiver.

▶ *Information to keep handy after registration:*

- Date you registered
- NCAA ID#
- Email address used to register
- High schools attended
- Date your six-semester transcript was sent
- Date your test score was sent
- Date your final transcript (with proof of graduation) was sent

ACADEMIC CERTIFICATION DECISIONS

In order to receive an academic certification, you must have:

- Your final transcript with proof of graduation
- Official transcripts from all high schools attended
- SAT and ACT test scores
- No open academic tasks

After submitting all of your information to the Eligibility Center, and being placed on a school's institutional request list (IRL), you will receive one of the following certifications from the NCAA:

DIVISION I

Early Academic Qualifier—if you meet specific criteria after six semesters of high school instead of the typical eight, you may be an early academic qualifier. You will be able to receive a scholarship, practice and compete in your first year of enrollment in college.

Qualifier—You will be able to receive a scholarship, practice and compete in your first year of enrollment in college.

Academic Redshirt—You may receive a scholarship and may practice in your first year of enrollment but you may not compete. You must pass either eight quarter or nine semester hours to practice in the next term.

Non-qualifier—You may not receive a scholarship, practice or compete.

DIVISION II

Early Academic Qualifier—If you meet specific criteria after six semesters of high school instead of the typical eight, you may be an early academic qualifier. You will be able to receive a scholarship, practice and compete in your first year of enrollment in college.

Qualifier—You will be able to receive a scholarship, practice and compete in your first year of enrollment in college.

Partial Qualifier—You may receive a scholarship and practice during your first year of enrollment but you may not compete.

Non-qualifier—You may not receive a scholarship, practice or compete.

Refer to the Division I and Division II sections for the qualifications of these certifications. Once a coach places you on their IRL, they will receive notification of your certification and subsequent eligibility.

| DIVISION I

Division I schools tend to have the largest student bodies, the largest athletic budgets and the most

athletic scholarships. There are about 350 schools participating at the DI level and approximately 59% of the athletes at these schools receive athletic scholarships.

The Ivy League Institutions are Division I schools, but they do not offer athletic or academic scholarships. You can only receive their generous need-based aid if you meet their academic requirements. The Ivy League consists of Brown, Columbia, Cornell, Dartmouth, Harvard, the University of Pennsylvania, Princeton and Yale.

▶ *Academic Requirements*

Student-athletes are required to meet certain academic standards in order to compete, practice, and receive a scholarship at an NCAA school. You need to complete the required number of NCAA-approved **core courses,** graduate from high school, and meet all of the following requirements:

> **Complete a total of 16 core courses**
> 4 years English
> 3 years Math
> 2 years Natural/Physical Science (1 year of lab if offered)
> 1 year additional either English/Math/Science
> 2 years Social Science
> 4 years additional courses
>   (Math, English, Natural/Physical Science, foreign language or comparative religion/philosophy)

Core course progression requirements:

1. **Complete 10 of your 16 core courses** including 7 in English, Math, Natural/Physical Science before the start of your seventh semester. This is known as the 10/7 requirement. Once you start your seventh semester. You must have more than 10 courses completed in order to repeat or replace any courses used to meet the 10/7 requirement.

2. **Complete the 16 NCAA-approved core courses in right academic semester** or four consecutive academic years from the start of ninth grade. If you graduate from high school early, you must still meet the core course requirements.

3. **Earn an SAT combined score or ACT sum score that matches your core course GPA** (minimum 2.300) on the Division I sliding scale. (to find the sliding scale, visit NCAA.org).

DIVISION I

▶ Athletic Eligibility

NCAA Eligibility Center Certification Decisions

You must receive an academic certification decision from the NCAA Eligibility Center that qualifies you to compete at the DI Level. To receive a certification decision, you must register for a certification account at eligibilitycenter.org and be placed on a school's institutional request list and have submitted all requirements to the Eligibility Center.

See page 42 for more information on an NCAA certification account

Qualifications for eligibility:

Early Academic Qualifier—if you meet specific criteria after six semesters of high school instead of the typical eight, you may be an early academic qualifier. You will be able to receive a scholarship, practice and compete in your first year of enrollment in college.

- Minimum SAT combined score (math and critical reading) of 900 OR minimum ACT sum score of 75
  - Core course GPA of 3.000 or higher in a minimum of 14 core courses:
  - English—3 years
  - Math—2 years
  - Natural/Physical Science—2 years
  - Two additional years of the courses above
  - Five additional core courses in any area (see core course section in this workbook)

Qualifier—If you meet the core course progression requirements for Division I, you will be able to receive a scholarship, practice and compete in your first year of enrollment in college.

Academic Redshirt—If you do not meet all of the DI academic standards, you may not compete in your first year of enrollment. However, you may receive a scholarship and practice in your first year of enrollment if you qualify as an academic redshirt. To do so, you must:

- Complete 16 core courses

- Earn an SAT combined score or ACT sum score matching your core course GPA (min. 2.000) on the

  DI sliding scale. The lower your GPA, the higher your test scores must be. (See NCAA.org to find the Division I sliding scale)

Non-qualifier—You have not met the academic standards and may not receive a scholarship, practice or compete in the NCAA.

See NCAA.org for the Division I Worksheet to help you keep track of your core courses throughout your high school career.

DIVISION I

▶ Scholarships

DI schools have the ability to offer full scholarships that include tuition, fees, room and board, books and certain fees related to courses. They may also offer partial scholarships that will cover some portion of these expenses. DI schools may offer athletes multi-year scholarships and they may also offer to pay for a student to finish their bachelor's or master's degrees after they have finished playing.

Conversely, if receiving a scholarship, **the amount can increase, decrease or be taken away fully every year.** If this happens, the school must notify you by July 1 and provide an opportunity to appeal.

Below is a chart that shows the full scholarship limits per sport for Division I. However, just because a sport **CAN** have this many scholarships available per the NCAA, does not mean that they **DO** have that many available per their institution. If you would like to know what the college you are interested in has available to them, ask the coach!

Scholarship Limits Per Sport

Men's Sports

Baseball	11.7
Basketball (Head Count)	13.0
Cross Country/Track	12.6
Fencing	4.5
Football- FBS (Head Count)	85.0
Football- FCS	63.0
Golf	4.5
Gymnastics	6.3
Ice Hockey	18.0
Lacrosse	12.6
Rifle (Includes Women)	3.6
Skiing	6.3
Soccer	9.9
Swimming/Diving	9.9
Tennis	4.5
Volleyball	4.5
Water Polo	4.5
Wrestling	9.9

Women's Sports

Basketball (Head Count)	15.0
Bowling	5.0
Cross Country/Track	18
Equestrian	15.0
Fencing	5.0
Field Hockey	12
Golf	6.0
Gymnastics (Head Count)	12.0
Ice Hockey	18.0
Lacrosse	12.0
Rowing	20.0
Rugby	12.0
Sand Volleyball	6.0
Skiing	7.0
Soccer	14.0
Softball	12.0
Swimming/Diving	14.0
Tennis (Head Count)	8.0
Volleyball Head Count)	12.0
Water Polo	8.0

DIVISION I

▶ *Recruiting Rules*

Division I coaches have to adhere to strict rules about contacting and recruiting prospective student-athletes. Additionally, each sport will vary in their recruiting calendar pertaining to quiet periods, dead periods, evaluation periods, etc. So be sure to rely on the coaches to follow the rules and keep you apprised of when they can and cannot have contact with you and your parents.

One thing to mention...you can contact a college coach at any time. Recruiting rules only limit when coaches can communicate with you.

Each sport has a different recruiting calendar with different timelines for dead periods, quiet periods, contact periods and evaluation periods. College coaches will know and adhere to their calendar.
You can refer to the recruiting chart included in this workbook for more specifics on each sport, but here are some basics for each year of your recruiting process **(check the chart for differences in these sports)**.

Division I Recruiting Rules by Year

SOPHOMORE YEAR
- You may call the coach any time but the coach may not call you **(lacrosse)**
- No off-campus contact
- No official visits
- Unlimited unofficial visits, except during a dead period **(wrestling, lacrosse, women's gymnastics)**

JUNIOR YEAR
- You may call the coach any time **(lacrosse)**
- The coach can call you starting Sept. 1st **(men's basketball, football, swimming & diving)**
- Electronic correspondence (email, text messages, etc.) may begin after Sept. 1st **(men's basketball)**
- Check your sport on the chart for off-campus contact rules
- No official visits **(men's and women's basketball, football)**
- Unlimited unofficial visits **(wrestling, lacrosse, women's gymnastics)**

SENIOR YEAR
- You may call the coach at any time
- All correspondence is allowed with some limitations placed on the number of times per week a coach can call you and the time of year based around their recruiting calendar. Coaches know these rules so athletes do not need to worry.
- Off-campus contact (home visit, evaluation, high school visit) can only be made three times before an NLI is signed. Unlimited after an NLI is signed **(men's and women's basketball, football)**
- Official visits allowed after your first day of classes. You may only take one per college to a maximum of five colleges.

DIVISION I

DIVISION II

Institutions at the NCAA Division II level try to **emphasize a life balance in which students can spend a little more time focusing on academics** while still competing in their sport at a high level. They will be able to have a traditional college experience while still being an athlete.

There are slightly more than 300 schools at the DII level and approximately 62% of athletes receive athletic scholarships.

▶ *Academic Requirements*

Student athletes are required to meet certain academic standards in order to compete, practice, and

receive a scholarship at an NCAA school. You need to complete the required number of NCAA-approved **core courses,** graduate from high school, and meet all of the following requirements:

1. **Complete a total of 16 core courses**
    3 years English
    2 years Math
    2 years Natural/Physical Science (1 year of lab if offered)
    3 year additional either English/Math/Science
    2 years Social Science
    4 years additional courses
      (Math, English, Natural/Physical Science, foreign language or comparative religion/philosophy)

2. Earn an SAT combined score or ACT sum score that matches your core course GPA (minimum 2.200) on the Division II sliding scale. The lower your GPA, the higher your test scores need to be. **(To find the sliding scale, visit NCAA.org)**

To understand more about the NCAA academic requirements in Division II, be sure to speak to your high school counselor, the college coach, or refer to NCAA.org.

DIVISION II

▶ Athletic Eligibility

NCAA Eligibility Center Certification Decisions

You must receive an academic certification decision from the NCAA Eligibility Center that qualifies you to compete at the DII Level. To receive a certification decision, you must register for a certification account at eligibilitycenter.org and be placed on a school's institutional request list and have submitted all requirements to the Eligibility Center.

See page 42 for more information on an NCAA certification account

Qualifications for eligibility:

Early Academic Qualifier—If you meet specific criteria after six semesters of high school instead of the typical eight, you may be an early academic qualifier. You will be able to receive a scholarship, practice and compete in your first year of enrollment in college.

- Minimum SAT combined score (math and critical reading) of 900 OR minimum ACT sum score of 68
- Core course GPA of 2.500 or higher in a minimum of 14 core courses:
    English—3 years
    Math—3 years
    Natural/Physical Science—2 years
    6 additional core courses in any area *(see core course section in this book)*

Qualifier—If you meet the core course progression requirements for Division II, *(see page or section)* you will be able to receive a scholarship, practice and compete in your first year of enrollment in college.

Partial Qualifier—If you do not meet all of the DII academic standards, you may not compete in your first year of enrollment. However, you may receive a scholarship and practice in your first year of enrollment if you are certified as a Partial Qualifier. To do so, you must:

- Complete 16 core courses
- Earn an SAT combined score or ACT sum score matching your core course GPA (min. 2.000) on the DII sliding scale. The lower your GPA, the higher your test scores must be. (See NCAA.org to find the Division I sliding scale)

Non-qualifier—You have not met the academic standards and may not receive a scholarship, practice or compete in the NCAA.

See NCAA.org for the Division II Worksheet to help you keep track of your core courses throughout your high school career.

DIVISION II

▶ Scholarships

Division II operates on a **partial-scholarship model for financial aid based on athletics**. There are not many DII student-athletes who receive full athletics grants, but 62% will receive at least some athletics-based financial aid.

DII scholarships are awarded as **equivalency grants** in which the coach and financial aid officers can take the number of full scholarships that they have available and split them amongst as many team members as they see fit. This, of course, means that not all team members will receive the same amount.

Below is a chart that shows the full scholarship limits per sport for Division II. However, just because a sport **CAN** have this many scholarships available per the NCAA, does not mean that the **DO** have that many available per their institution. If you would like to know what the college you are interested in has available to them, ask the coach!

Equivalency Limits Per Sport

Men's Sports

Baseball	9.0
Basketball	10.0
Cross Country/Track	12.6
Football	36.0
Fencing	4.5
Golf	3.6
Gymnastics	5.4
Ice Hockey	13.5
Lacrosse	10.8
Rifle	3.6
Skiing	6.3
Soccer	9.0
Swimming/Diving	8.1
Tennis	4.5
Volleyball	4.5
Water Polo	4.5
Wrestling	9.0

Women's Sports

Basketball	10.0
Bowling	5.0
Cross Country/Track	12.6
Equestrian	15.0
Fencing	4.5
Field Hockey	6.3
Golf	5.4
Gymnastics	6.0
Ice Hockey	18.0
Lacrosse	9.0
Rowing	20.0
Rugby	12.0
Sand Volleyball	5.0
Skiing	6.3
Soccer	9.9
Softball	7.2
Swimming/Diving	8.1
Tennis	6.0
Volleyball	8.0
Water Polo	8.0

DIVISION II

Recruiting Rules

Recruiting rules in Division II are a little bit more straight forward than Division I:

- You may call the coach at any time
- The coach can call you any time after June 15 before senior year
- Unlimited number of off-campus contacts after June 15 before senior year
- Unlimited number of unofficial visits except during dead periods
- You may only make one official visit per college but may visit as many colleges as you like

Remember...
Each sport has a different recruiting calendar with different timelines for dead periods, quiet periods, contact periods and evaluation periods. College coaches will know and adhere to their calendar.

My Notes:

DIVISION II

DIVISION III

The primary focus of Division III student-athletes is their education. DIII presents the best life balance in college because of shorter playing seasons, which allow them to participate in other campus activities, and spend more time on their studies.

DIII has the most institutions in the NCAA at almost 450. Although you cannot receive an athletic scholarship from a DIII school, **about 80% of student-athletes in this division receive non-athletics aid** in the form of academic scholarships or need-based aid.

Division III is often considered the "lowest level" of competition, but DIII athletics are still highly competitive. There are high and low levels in every division and some DIII schools can beat some DII and lower level DI schools. So don't count out Division III as a great option even if you want to play at a high level!

▶ Academic Requirements

To be eligible to play at a Division III school, athletes must simply meet the academic requirements established by the institution to be considered for admission. Student-athletes cannot receive preferential consideration or have different academic standards than the general pool of applicants.

▶ Athletic Eligibility

You do not need to register with the NCAA Eligibility Center to play at the DIII level. You must only be able to be accepted to the institution under the same academic requirements as the general student body.

▶ Scholarships

Although you may not receive any scholarship money related to your athletic ability in Division III, many students receive more money through academic scholarships and need-based aid than they would have received in athletic scholarships at the DI or DII levels.

▶ Recruiting Rules

Recruiting rules in DIII become a lot more lenient. This is to give student-athletes the chance to get to know smaller schools better to help them make an informed decision. Also, being able to contact recruits sooner and more often gives the coaches a little bit of an advantage over their DI and DII colleagues who have the ability to offer scholarships to incent prospects to their schools. The basic Division III recruiting rules are:

- Unlimited calls from the coach at any time
- Unlimited off-campus contacts after sophomore year
- One official visit per school starting Jan.1st of their junior year to an unlimited number of schools.

Time Commitment per Division

Average number of ATHLETIC hours per week during athletic season

Div I - 33 hours
Div II - 31 hours
Div III - 28 hours

Football and baseball average 2-4 athletic hours more per week across all divisions

Average number of ACADEMIC hours per week during athletic season

Div I - 35 hours
Div II - 35 hours
Div III - 37 hours

Women's sports average 3-5 academic hours more per week across all divisions

*According to an NCAA survey

CONTACT RULES

Each sport and division has a different recruiting calendar with different timelines for dead periods, quiet periods, contact periods and evaluation periods. College coaches will know and adhere to their calendar.

Below is a **basic** overview of the different contact rules by division. Coaches will also know these contact rules and will be able to tell you when they can and cannot communicate with you.

Contact rules chart

Coach Action	NCAA		
	DI	DII	DIII
When can a coach email you?	Beginning June 15, immediately preceding your Junior year in high school		Unrestricted once you begin 9th grade
When can a coach call you?			
How often can a coach call you?	Unlimited during contact period		
When can a coach speak with you off campus?	Beginning June 15, immediately preceding your Junior year in high school	Begins June 15 PRIOR to 11th Grade	Upon completion of 10th grade
When can a coach speak with you at events?	*Last* day of an event after completion of competition and you have been 'released' by your coach		*Any* day of an event after completion of competition and you have been 'released' by your coach
When is a coach's quiet period? (Can only have face to face contact on campus.)	The NCAA has separate calendars that affect each governed sport. Consult ncaa.org for your sport.	Only football and basketball have quiet periods. All other sports do not have quiet periods.	None
When is a coach's dead period? (No face to face contact allowed.)		The NCAA has separate calendars for each governed sport. Consult ncaa.org.	

Coach Action	NAIA	NJCAA
	DI & DII	DI DII & DIII
When can a coach email you?	Anytime	Anytime
When can a coach call you?	Anytime	Anytime
How often can a coach call you?	Unlimited	Unlimited
When can a coach speak with you off campus?	Unlimited	Unlimited
When can a coach speak with you at tournaments?	Unlimited	Unlimited
When is a coach's quiet period? (Can only have face to face contact on campus.)	None	None
When is a coach's dead period? (No face to face contact allowed.)	None	None

Additional Information

Recruit Action	NCAA		
	DI*	DII	DIII
When can you make an unofficial visit?	Any time but may not speak with coaches during Dead Periods		First day of 9th grade
When can you make an official visit?	8/1 of Junior year	June 15 prior to 11th grade	After January 1st of 11th grade
When can you participate in a tryout?	Beginning of season after enrollment	June 15 PRIOR 11th grade; not during HS season	Beginning of season after enrollment
Other restrictions	Need NCAA Eligibility Center Certification Account in order to go on official visits or sign an NLI		Registration in NCAA Eligibility Center is NOT required
Scholarships can include up to:	Tuition, fees, housing, meals, books, and cost of living stipend.	Tuition, fees, housing, meals, books	Academic scholarships only
1st Day Scholarships man be signed (National Letter of Intent)	NLI: Early Signing Period is one week in mid-November during 12th grade, Regular Signing Period starts in mid-April		There is no NLI; celebratory letter may be provided once the student has been accepted
Sports-specific calendars	The NCAA has specific calendars for the following sports: football, baseball basketball, cross country, track & field, golf, lacrosse, volleyball, beach volleyball, softball and other sports. You should consult the NCAA recruiting calendars at http://www.ncaa.org/student-athletes/resources/recruiting-calendars.		

*DI Service Academy rule can be found at NCAA.org

Recruit Action	NAIA	NJCAA		
	DI & DII	DI	DII	DIII
When can you make an unofficial visit?	Anytime (no difference between official/unofficial)	Anytime		
When can you make an official visit?	Anytime	Anytime		
When can you participate in a tryout?	Anytime, twice per school, not during high school season	Anytime, once per school, not during HS season		
Other restrictions	Registration in NAIA Clearinghouse is required	Can not be your club coach if a signed player		
Scholarships can include up to:	Tuition, fees, books, supplies,housing and meals	Tuition, fees, books, housing, potential summer tuition	Tuition, fees, books, potential summer tuition	Academic scholarships only
1st Day Scholarships may be signed (National Letter of Intent)	Varies by school	November 1 of 12th grade season		

My NCAA Notes:

The College
RECRUITING PROCESS

Your College Recruiting Project

Define what you want to gain along your journey, then begin!

There is a saying, *"Plan the work, then work the plan"*. The journey begins with you contemplating the life you would like to live, then determining the path on how to achieve that overall goal.

For example, think about having a house, a car, vacationing every year. Then start asking how big of a house? What kind of car? What kind of vacations? Once you have answered those questions, start adding dollar values to them. How much do they cost to get? How much do they cost to maintain? Total all of those numbers and now you have an idea of how much money it will take to live that lifestyle.

Once you have calculated the amount of money it will take to achieve, then maintain, your chosen lifestyle then you can start thinking about the kinds of careers you would need to have to achieve those goals and maintain them. Keep in mind your lifestyle decisions are not set in stone and are meant to be adjusted over time, but thinking like this gives you a more direct path to follow on your journey.

From those careers, you can begin to contemplate the education you would need to have in order to obtain those jobs. Then you can focus on what kind of school you want to attend. Is it large, medium or small? Is it diverse? Is it located in a big city, the suburbs or a rural community? Does it have your sport? Etc.

Now you're ready for what's next!

- Things to consider about colleges
- Yearly tasks
- Contacting coaches
- Recruiting videos
- Campus visits
- Questions to ask

THINGS TO CONSIDER WHEN LOOKING FOR & CHOOSING A COLLEGE

Everyone has different priorities when they are researching and choosing their college. Some student-athletes only care about the institutional level they will play (*"I must play DI!"*) while others are more focused on still playing competitively at a high level—but only if they can receive the type of education they are looking for. Some aren't worried as much about the level of physical play, as long as they will be on the court or field during games, while others would be happy to be on the bench if they are part of a winning program or a large school. Everyone has their own priorities and it is **up to you to figure out** what yours are, and then make sure the college that you choose can meet those criteria.

Below is a list of things you might want to consider when choosing your school as a student-athlete. Some of these things may mean nothing to you or you may have other priorities not listed here. It may be helpful to rank all of these items in order of what you feel is the most important thing to have in your college experience to the least important. This will help guide you toward the right type of schools to when starting your search, and also help you ask the right questions to find our which school meets your ideals.

Take a minute to think about the items on this list and then put your top 5 most important priorities—in order of importance—in your own list on the right.

Education Level
Name of school - Recognition
Intended Major
Diversity
Job placement after graduation
Alumni network
Faculty/Student Ratio
Cost/Loans
Coach
Team
Scholarship
Team or School Culture
Playing Time
Winning
Level—DI, DII, DIII, etc.
School/Athletics Balance
Social Life
Extracurricular opportunities (Greek life, clubs, study abroad, etc.)

TOP 5 COLLEGE PRIORITIES

1. _____

2. _____

3. _____

4. _____

5. _____

Remember that these priorities may change for you throughout your college search! Keep updating your list whenever you feel that something is different!

THE RECRUITING PROCESS

YEAR-TO-YEAR

EVERY YEAR
√ **Review your lifestyle goals** √ **Review your career interests** √ **Get good grades!!**
√ Learn and improve your time management between academics and athletics
√ Be aware of your social media presence- coaches will check and they are looking for people of good character!
√ Get involved in your community- volunteer, raise money, help out!
√ Play at the highest level that you can, get good instruction, be coachable!
√ Track your grades and extracurricular activities (clubs, philanthropy, etc.) so you can include them on your applications
√ Talk to your guidance counselor to make sure your courses qualify for the NCAA.
√ Communicate with coaches- stay on their radar!!

8TH GRADE
√ **Review your lifestyle goals**
√ **Review your career interests**
√ **Keep your grades high!**
√ Talk to your high school guidance counselor when setting up classes to make sure that they know that you are interested in taking classes that would allow you to play a sport in college.
√ Start working on time management to be a student AND an athlete!

FRESHMAN YEAR
√ **Review your lifestyle goals**
√ **Review your career interests**
√ **Keep your grades high!**
√ Learn how to be a high level student AND athlete
√ Pay attention to academics- every grade from here on out will go on your official transcript
√ Consult with your guidance counselor to make sure your courses will qualify as NCAA Core Courses
√ Start using the NCAA Core Course Worksheet
√ Work hard in the classroom AND in your sport to excel at both- what you do now lays the foundation and will dictate what opportunities you have later
√ Be involved in your community
√ Be aware of what you are posting on social media
√ Start a list of colleges that you think you are interested in and research them
√ Start a list of your extracurricular activities— volunteering, philanthropy, clubs, etc. so that you can list them on your applications.

THE RECRUITING PROCESS

CHECKLIST

SOPHOMORE YEAR
√ **Review your lifestyle goals** √ **Review your career interests** √ **Keep your grades high!**
√ Research colleges- start with a broad list of any school that interests you. Start to think about what experiences you are looking for in college.
√ Create an NCAA and NAIA Eligibility Center Profile if you plan to look at or be recruited by any DI, DII or NAIA schools.
√ Consult with your guidance counselor to take NCAA-approved Core Courses
√ Start preparing for SAT and/or ACT Tests
√ Start attending college camps and ID clinics
√ Email coaches to introduce yourself and let them know of your interest. Include your video, academic goals and your playing schedule.
√ Set up phone calls with college coaches to ask them questions about their programs and have them get to know you better.

JUNIOR YEAR
√ **Review your lifestyle goals**
√ **Review your career interests**
√ **Keep your grades high!**
√ Take SAT or ACT tests early in the school year so that you have an opportunity to improve upon them if necessary.
√ Take highest level classes that you can succeed in (AP and Honors if possible)
√ Know where you stand financially to pay for college. Figure out your Expected Family Contribution (EFC) and use the Net Price Calculators on your top college's websites.
√ Start taking unofficial campus visits. Talk to the coaches while there if you are allowed.
√ Update your video regularly and send to coaches along with your playing schedule.
√ Talk to coaches about where you stand on their recruiting list.
√ Attend ID Clinics and Summer Camps of your top schools.

SENIOR YEAR
√ **Review your lifestyle goals**
√ **Review your career interests**
√ **Keep your grades high!**
√ Narrow your search to your 3-5 top schools based on the experience you are looking for.
√ Take official visits within the number allotted
√ Respond to all coaches still interested and consider any offers you are given
√ Fill out FAFSA and any other financial aid documents.
√ Fill out applications to your top 3-5 schools completely and by their deadline. You can never be too sure that you are definitely getting in unless you have documentation from the school.
√ Complete all tasks for the NCAA and NAIA Eligibility Centers if necessary.
√ MAKE YOUR CHOICE based on academics, athletics and finances.

CONTACTING COLLEGES

Coaches do not often spend time reading and responding to generic emails that are obviously mass emails. Unless you have stats that are through the roof and are a super stud that can catch their eye, chances are that they will not respond to you from a mass email unless their school is highly specialized and your criteria matches theirs, or they are desperate for players.

Unless the coach has contacted you first, **they want to know that you are truly interested** in exploring their school as a real possibility before they take the time to invest in developing a relationship with you. Plus, it saves time on both ends if you have already researched the school to see if it has your major (if you know it), to understand the academic requirements to be accepted, and to know the cost of the school and whether your family would be able to afford it with or without scholarships and aid.

Here are a few tips to keep in mind when contacting a coach:

Tip 1: Before You Contact

- Make sure your email address does not reflect your fifth grade self! Although receiving an email from *puppiez4life@aol.com* would be comical to a coach, it is definitely not professional and leaves the door open for the coach to make an immediate judgment - good or bad. Create a new recruiting email address **THAT YOU WILL CHECK OFTEN** if necessary.
- Write professionally and respectfully.
- Use complete sentences and do not shorten words.
- Use spell-check!

Tip 2: Initial Contact

- Send an introductory email to the head and assistant coaches. Bigger schools may have position coaches and/or recruiting coordinators, too. Check school websites for up-to-date contact information.
- Always include your grad year, position, and a video in your initial contact with coaches
- **MAKE IT PERSONAL!**
    - *Tell the coach why you are interested in their school in particular*
    - *Why are you a good fit for their program?*

THE RECRUITING PROCESS

- Include your stats if you have them
- Include your academic information—GPA and test scores. You do not need to send transcripts unless the coach requests them.
- Include your playing schedule and ask if they will be at any events that you are attending
- Include your club and/or high schools coach's contact information, but make sure to let your current coach know that you are doing so and ask what contact info they would like you to give out.

Tip 3: Follow-Up

- If you don't hear back immediately, **follow up with another email in a few weeks.** It may be a busy time of year for a coach or a period of the recruiting calendar in which they cannot respond.
- Continue to let the coach know what events you are attending and where you can be seen.
- Update the coaching staff with video as often as you can.

Tip 4: What Not To Do

- **DO NOT** harass a coach or continue to email them if they have not contacted you. Stay in touch and drop them a line with updated video every so often.
- **DO NOT** approach coaches when they are recruiting at your event. Chances are they cannot talk o you per NCAA rules and they don't like to be rude and tell you they can't talk.
- **DO NOT** write to coaches in "text speak" or without proper grammar or punctuation. Remember, they are evaluating whether you will be successful in college.
- **DO NOT** show up to campus unannounced. Let the coach know ahead of time that you plan to visit campus and when you are coming and schedule a time to meet.

The biggest key to contact:
COMMUNICATION

Always respond to a coach's email, text or phone call! The best way to be dropped from a college's radar is to show a lack of interest and initiative.

THE RECRUITING PROCESS

My Notes About Recruiting Timeline and Contacting Coaches:

RECRUITING VIDEO
Information

SKILLS

- Typically in practice or at a showcase or combine where you perform skills in a controlled drill
- Can help the coach see your mastery of a specific skill
- Start with with your best skill that is most important to your position

VS.

HIGHLIGHTS

- Clips from game play that showcase your ability or talent
- Usually your very best plays. Be sure to show what lead up to your highlight and the result
- Show plays from multiple skills of the game to show your versatility

VS.

GAME PLAY

- Video of a full game (or portions of one)
- Cut out portions where you are not playing, did not perform your skill, and all dead time between plays (i.e. football setting up for the next play)
- Allows coaches to see your ability within the context of the game

Why have a video?

- Allows coaches to assess your ability and possible impact on their team without having to travel to see you play.

- Allows you to reach out to coaches across the country instead of waiting until they are able to see you play in person. Gives you a much larger list of schools that you could get interested in you.

- Most coaches in this digital age expect to see video in order to decide whether or not to put you on, keep you on, or add you to their radar.

- Coaches often will not respond to a recruit that has emailed them and not included a video.

- A good video will grab a coach's attention and make them remember you.

- You should always include a video in any correspondence with a coach—especially your first one.

- You can update your video regularly to send to a coach to demonstrate your improvement and continued interest in their school.

THE RECRUITING PROCESS

Tips for making your recruiting video

- Know what college coaches in your sport are looking for. You can ask!

- Make it short, sweet and to the point- 3-5 minutes tops. Odds are that the coach will not watch the whole thing either way, but they are definitely not going to spend 10 minutes watching every play you were in the whole season. So be selective!

- Put your best stuff first! Always start your video with your very best plays first. You need to grab the coach's attention and make them want to watch more of your video.

- Make sure to always start your video with clips in the position that you want to be recruited to play. For example, if you are a volleyball player who wants to be recruited as a hitter, do not start your video with clips of you serving or playing defense. You may still add those later (no more than a minute each maybe) but start it out with your best hits.

- Use arrows or spot shadows. Before the action, make sure that the coach can find you in the play but do not stop the action in the middle of your movement.

- Add time before and after your part of the play. Depending on your sport, be sure to show what leads up to your play and the outcome.

- Have high quality video if possible.

- Showcase all of the skills that you possess in your sport, but again, always start with your primary position or skill set.

- Start the video with all of your information, either written or spoken. Include your name, high school and/or club, graduation year, position and jersey number at least. You may also include your GPA and other academic accolades if looking at high academic schools.

- Upload your video to BeSeenSports, YouTube Hudl or Vimeo and send the link to coaches.

- Update your video often with new footage to send to coaches throughout the recruiting process.

Tip:

DO NOT USE INAPPROPRIATE MUSIC FOR YOUR VIDEO!

It may sound cool to you, but think about your audience. The music you choose will allow the coach to make a judgment about you and your character. So if you choose inappropriate and disrespectful music, coaches will automatically assume you are a disrespectful player.

My Notes About Making My Video:

THE CAMPUS VISIT

> *When meeting with a coach on your first visit to their school, it's important to make it memorable for them and to leave a good impression so they are encouraged to keep you on their radar. Here are a few ways that could make you stand out from the many other recruits they are talking to in your position.*

DRESS FOR SUCCESS

Make sure that you do not show up in sweatpants and sports attire. (Especially not from another college!) Business casual is appropriate for the occasion because you will also likely be meeting with college admissions counselors, interacting with professors, meeting the team and perhaps meeting other members of the athletic staff. This really is an interview after all!

RESEARCH THE SCHOOL AND THE TEAM

Make sure that you have a lot of information about the school and the team. Coaches appreciate when their recruit has taken time to learn about their school academically and athletically as it shows an investment in the recruiting process with them.

ASK GREAT QUESTIONS

Prepare insightful questions, like the ones provided in this book, to ask the coach during your visit. Coaches really appreciate when the athlete asks questions about the team, the coach, the institution, etc. For one, it gives them a chance to talk about their program and school without sounding like they are only trying to sell you something. Second, your questions tell them about your priorities in selecting a school. There is almost nothing worse than when a coach is done with their sales pitch and they ask if you have any questions and you say "No, not really".

THE CAMPUS VISIT

GIVE GREAT ANSWERS
Be prepared to confidently answer questions about yourself. A coach is going to ask you questions that give you an opportunity to discuss your strengths and weaknesses, athletic and academic goals, and your previous athletic experiences, to name a few possibilities. You will need to provide concise answers that allow the coach to get to know you while also showing them how serious you are about being a college athlete and team player.

SPEAK FOR YOURSELF
Make sure that YOU answer all questions that the coach asks, not your parents. Coaches are recruiting you, not your family. They may ask specific questions to your parents, which they should obviously answer, but when a parent overwhelms the conversation and does not allow their child to speak for themselves, it leaves a very bad impression on the coach. You will be remembered as the recruit who didn't say anything or the one with the overbearing parents as opposed to the really good wide receiver.

BE YOURSELF
Don't try to be someone else on your college visit. Be yourself and answer the questions in the way that you really feel. Putting on a false front for a coach or the team will not allow them to get to know you like they should. No coach expects perfection and they know that you will bring certain strengths and weaknesses along with you, but they want to hear your plan to improve and contribute to their program.

BE APPRECIATIVE
Always thank a coach for their time and effort in arranging your campus visit. If you leave the college with a good impression and feel as though you would still like to pursue the possibility of joining their team, feel free to send a follow-up email, or even a hand-written note, to thank them and tell them what you liked about your visit.

UNOFFICIAL VS. OFFICIAL VISITS

Official

- You may only have ONE official visit at any institution

- Total number of official visits are limited in DI and DII- make sure you keep track of your official visits iand choose your visits wisely!

- Some divisions may require transcripts, test scores and eligibility center registration before visiting

- Cannot be longer than 48 hours

- The institution can pay for many expenses for you and your parents or guardians including meals, transportation and reasonable entertainment expenses- amounts vary by division

Unofficial

- Can make an unlimited amount of unofficial visits at any time (exceptions in DI and DII lacrosse, wrestling and women's gymnastics).

- Cannot talk to a coach on campus during a dead period

- DI and DII can provide certain amounts of tickets to home athletic contests

- You pay your own expenses

See the Collegiate Athletic Association section of this book for more specific recruiting rules per division about official and unofficial visits.

THE CAMPUS VISIT

QUESTIONS *to ask the coach on a phone call or campus visit...*

We have compiled a list of possible questions for you to ask the coach either over the phone or while on a campus visit. Be sure to ask questions that are relevant to the school you are visiting (i.e. don't ask a DIII school about athletic scholarships). These are only suggestions—choose those questions most important to you and your college experience. ALWAYS BE PREPARED WITH QUESTIONS!! Coaches do not enjoy prospective athletes who say they have nothing to ask!!!

Academics

- What are your academic expectations?
- Do you have any say in the admissions process?
- What is your policy with academic conflicts?
- What percentage of your athletes graduate in four years?
- What is the team GPA?
- What type of academic support is offered to your athletes?
- What is the average class size?
- Do athletes miss any classes due to your travel or game schedule? Can those be made up? Are they excused?
- How do the professors here feel about student-athletes?
- Do they support them academically and give alternatives for missed class time?
- What are your policies around academics interfering with athletics?
- Do you have an academic advising center? How many players use it?
- How many credits do I need to be eligible to play?
- What are your academic requirements to keep my scholarship? Financial Aid?

THE CAMPUS VISIT

Sport

- Where do I fit into your roster and what position will I play?
- Have you seen me play live or watched my video? If so, in your opinion, what can I improve upon to best fit your needs?
- What are your practices like?
- What is the practice and game schedule?
- What is the typical day like for your student-athletes?
- What is the off-season like?
- When does the season start? End?
- What is a typical day in-season and out-of-season?
- What do your current players do well in order to earn playing time?
- How many freshmen are you recruiting in my position?
- Do I have a chance to earn playing time as a freshmen?
- Where am I on your recruiting list for my position?
- Does the team work out? What is their training schedule like outside of practice?
- How do you determine whether or not someone will redshirt for a year and why?
- What are the physical requirements to play (i.e., training, weight, speed, tests, etc.)?
- How far do you travel in your conference?
- Do most of your players stay on the team all four years?
- Do you make cuts? If so, how do you make those decisions?
- Once I'm on the team, do I remain on the team or do I "tryout" every year?
- What happens if I get injured?
- Do you take walk-ons? If so, how do they fit into the team? Are they treated differently? How many do you have now?
- What are your athlete's summer obligations?
- Do you have a camp? Does attending the camp increase my odds of being on the team?
- What support do you get in terms of attendance from the student body?
- How would your team describe your coaching style?
- How long have you been coaching here? Does your coaching contract end while I will be a student-athlete here?
- Do you have any plans to leave in the near future?
- What is your philosophy on playing time?
- What is your sideline demeanor during games?
- What are the responsibilities of your assistants in the program?
- What is the current status of the college's relationship with the NCAA?

THE CAMPUS VISIT

Team

- Where do the majority of your players come from, geographically?
- What is the role/expectations of your captains/leadership?
- What are the team's biggest accomplishments in the last 5 years?
- Do you do any philanthropy as a team?
- Are you involved in the community in any way?
- What are your expectations for team conduct?
- Do you allow dual sport athletes on your team?
- What activities do you do as a team?
- How does your team get along?
- What is unique about your team?
- How do you choose captains?
- What is your discipline philosophy?
- What are the college's conduct rules?
- Is there a JV Team? How does that work?
- Does the team live together?
- Are your student-athletes able to study abroad?
- Can I be involved in other organizations on campus like sororities, fraternities, clubs, etc.? What are your expectations for that?

College

- What is the average class size?
- What majors are your players involved in?
- Do the professors support athletes?
- Is athletics well-supported by the administration?
- How does playing on a team affect my class time?
- How much class time will I miss during season?
- What is the graduation rate of your team?
- Are there research opportunities on campus?
- What clubs/organizations are your team members involved in?
- Is this school known as a party school?
- What is Greek life like on campus, and are team members involved?

Financial Aid/Scholarships

- Will I receive a written contract if I receive a scholarship?
- How do you award scholarships? Can they be taken away?
- Is there potential to increase my scholarship amount in the future based on performance?
- What expenses does a scholarship cover? Tuition, room, board, books supplies, etc.?
- Is financial aid available for summer school?
- If injured, what happens to my scholarship/financial aid?
- Is there work study that can help me offset costs? Are your student-athletes allowed to have on-campus jobs?
- Does the college cover medical expenses or do I need to have my own insurance?
- What is your average financial aid package?
- What is the typical breakdown of loans versus grants?
- What percentage of financial need does the school typically meet?
- What is the average college debt that students leave with?

My Questions:

And lastly, always ask…

Where do I stand on your recruiting list? Is there anything else you need from me right now? What is the next step in the recruiting process for me?

THE CAMPUS VISIT

PARENTS: WHAT TO DO

1. *Do* encourage your son/daughter to be proactive in the recruiting process.
2. *Do* help them to keep their academic and athletic resume up-to-date.
3. *Do* remind them regularly how important their grades are if they want to play in college.
4. *Do* take video of their games and help them edit their highlight film or hire a service to do so.
5. *Do* talk with them about why they are leaning toward one school or another and help them think through them decision-making process.
6. *Do* help hem to fill out recruiting questionnaires and craft an email to send to coaches— **HELP them! Do not do it for them!**
7. *Do* assist them in planning college visits.
8. *Do* let them know how much you are willing, if any, to contribute to their college education.
9. *Do* make sure they fill out all college and scholarship applications before deadlines.

PARENTS: WHAT *NOT* TO DO

1. *Don't* pressure your child to receive a scholarship or choose YOUR favorite school
2. *Don't* fill out all college information and questionnaires for them.
3. *Don't* communicate with coaches for them
4. *Don't* email or call the coaches on your own.
5. *Don't* answer questions for them while on a college visit. The coach wants to hear from your son/daughter...not from you!
6. *Don't* try to "talk up" or exaggerate your child's athletic or academic ability to the coach. They will make up their mind on their own regardless of how great you think your child is!
7. *Don't* seem like an over-involved parent. If coaches perceive you as the type of parent who will continue to be too involved after the recruiting process, you may hurt your child's chances of making the team.
8. *Don't* make the final decision for your child. Ultimately, they have to live with the choice that they make, not you. Discuss each school academically, athletically and especially financially so that they have the full scope of their decision, but let them make it.

Do I need a recruiting service?

The PROS

A place to house your information

Will send emails on your behalf to schools that match your college profile criteria

They can often help you make your recruiting video, but they will likely charge a separate fee.

May provide important information on colleges

May provide a website to send to coaches

Introduce you to colleges based on your search criteria

Articles on recruiting and the college process

The CONS

Potentially high costs

Generic emails from recruiting sites may not be looked at by coaches

May be inundated with solicitation to purchase unnecessary add-ons

Not having control over your own process

Coaches may receive promotions for other athletes on the site, taking attention from you

Recruiters may push a certain school or level for their reputation

WHAT DO I NEED TO GET THE JOB DONE?

If you had to add up all of the hours that you have spent dedicating your time to your sport, you would be amazed by the astronomical number you would see! Put together **practices, games, travel time, workouts, individual sessions, watching film and meeting with coaches**, it could be more than full-time job. Not to mention the amount of money spent to give you that opportunity.

So what is on the other end of all of that time, effort and energy? Why are you doing all of this? What is the return on your investment for everything that you have sacrificed to play? Many student-athletes and parents will say that they are doing it all to open opportunities on the other end—in the form of playing in college.

It may be out of sheer necessity because a family would not be able to afford college without a scholarship. Or it could just be that you really enjoy playing the sport and want to continue to do so as long as you can while you get an education. ***The good news…***there are schools out there that can fit every kind of experience a student-athlete is looking for.

The bad news…somehow you have to find that school. And there are thousands of options out there! The recruiting process is often confusing and can feel daunting. So recruiting services have been born out of necessity to help families navigate these waters. The thing you have to ask yourself about recruiting services is:

What do I actually need?

The fact of the matter is—**no one NEEDS a recruiting service**. All of the information and resources that you really need are right at your fingertips as long as you have an internet connection! You can make a video, email coaches, research schools and make a decision without spending a dime on a service.

While it is possible, it certainly isn't easy.

Again, the college recruiting process is a long-term project. As with all projects, you need the right tools to collect and store information. Having a tool, like BeSeenSports™, can provide you a single space to store and review all of the information you collect is key. Below are a few things you will have to start to work on.

- Careers you are interested in
- The education you will need for those respective careers
- Specifics about colleges that have the education needed for those careers
- The tasks you have to get done along your journey
- The events you will tell coaches about
- A complete website showcasing your academic and athletic abilities

RECRUITING SERVICES

Once you have the right tools, you are ready to determine if you need a service. First, you have to figure out how much your time is worth to you in the long run. Doing all of those things on your own can be time-consuming (this is why we advise building a team around you). As we've established, you are already spending significant amounts of your time within your academics and athletics. So, getting the right kind of help to guide you through the process could be an option. Just remember there is nothing they can do that you cannot do yourself or with the help of your team.

Keep in mind the most important aspect of the process is that IT MUST BE DRIVEN BY THE STUDENT-ATHLETE.

YOU should be invested in finding the right school for you.
YOU should research schools yourself—whether you found them, a recruiting service found them, or they found you. Check them out for yourself!
YOU need to be responsible for making a decision this big because it's the first step to the rest of your life.

Finding the right college can absolutely be a scary process, but after juggling all you have for as long as you have, you can handle it! It's all about managing time and prioritizing tasks. These are things student-athletes are already great at!

More good news! Just like there are all different levels of college athletics experiences, there are many different levels of recruiting services as well. Each of them obviously will cost you a certain amount of money (and still cost you some time), but you have the ability to decide what is right for your college search, and your wallet!

RECRUITING SERVICES

RECRUITING SERVICES

Things to Consider if Choosing a Service

1. Not all services are created equal

Do your research on what it is you need to help with for your search. You can save a lot of money by putting in some elbow grease, but some people want more of a full-service kind of approach. Some services will continue to ask for more money for more services.

2. Coaches do not want to hear from the service.

Nowadays, coach's inboxes are inundated with recruiting emails. They often just delete the ones from services that are impersonal. They want to know that YOU are interested in their school – not that a computer thinks you're a good match.

3. Match tools may save time, open opportunities

A criteria-matching tool can be beneficial to you. Being able to search schools based on a major or an academic level or division level will help you find schools you had never known existed and could be the perfect match!

4. More is not always more

A lot of services offer free accounts. Then they spam you with all of the add-on service offerings (videos, more emails sent for you, etc.). Making you think you "need" them for the site to work the best for your "needs", but they almost always cost extra money!

5. Be realistic

While recruiting services can possibly be helpful and guide you through how to be recruited, they cannot convince coaches to take a player they do not want. If you have poor grades or a bad attitude, are disrespectful or just not great at your sport, recruiting services cannot change that. They may put you in front of a coach, but that coach makes the final decision.

Approaches to managing your project

Do-It-Yourself Tools

Do-It-Yourself tools, like those found at BeSeenSports™, operate on the premise that you will be doing the leg work. They encourage you to use the tools they have developed to make it easier to conduct your own research, contact coaches through your own email and schedule phone calls and visits yourself. They believe the fact that the recruiting process needs to be driven by the student-athlete by really digging into the recruiting process and finding out about a school and their sports program on their own.

▶ What you typically get:

- A searchable database of universities, colleges and vocational schools
- A list of tasks that need to be done each year
- A place to track all of your awards, extracurriculars, grades and career aspirations to help stay organized for when you apply to college
- A professional website with your academic and athletic information and your videos to share with coaches
- A place to keep your notes on careers, colleges, tasks, etc.
- A secure messaging system when coaches contact you via your website
- A searchable database for college coaches where they can find new recruits

▶ Be Aware:

- These services do not send emails out to coaches
- Sometimes have add-ons for an additional charge
- You have to be self-driven to get the most out of this tools

Personal Recruiters

Personal recruiters can be hired to pay attention specifically to the needs of the student-athlete. They are typically more expensive, but do come with some advantages.

▶ *What you typically get:*

- Save you time typically spent searching on your own
- Contacts with college coaches across the country
- Will search for colleges based on your specific priorities and criteria
- Have NCAA knowledge and will help you follow recruiting rules
- Should be able to help make a video and send to coaches
- Can help narrow down what you are looking for in your college experience
- May help you navigate the Admissions and Financial Aid processes as well

▶ *Be aware:*

- Can be quite costly
- Can have a reputation for promoting some colleges above others instead of your ideal college
- Handing the process over to someone else is not in the best interest of every student-athlete

Traditional Recruiting Services

Online recruiting services can provide a great presentation in the form of a nice web page on their website. They can also provide coaches with a searchable database where they can find athletes based on their own criteria. They can also offer a lot of information in the form of free articles as well as paid individual coaching. Most offer a basic free profile to start out and then advertise fee-based services.

▶ *What you typically get:*

- A page on their site you can share with coaches
- Searchable college database to tag the colleges you are interested in
- Send emails with your profile to coaches and programs that match your profile
- Often have lots of great recruiting articles
- Database for coaches to search for athletes
- Select colleges to solicit based on your predetermined criteria

▶ *Be aware:*

- Can be costly - free platforms often turn into solicitation for more fee-based services
- Emails to coaches might include other athletes—taking the full attention away from you
- Coaches may ignore impersonal emails from recruiting services

My Notes About Recruiting Tools and Services:

The BeSeenSports Method

At BeSeenSports we have a specific method that not only helps to identify appropriate schools to research, but also prepares you for how you can manage your chosen career once you graduate. We show you our 4 stages below where you plan in one direction and then execute in the other. Starting with your desired lifestyle you plan backwards and then execute in the opposite direction. This method gives you a clear path for achieving your goals.

PLAN   EXECUTE

1 — *Lifestyle*: Think about the lifestyle you want to have (house, car, vacations, etc.). Then put a dollar figure to it. — **4**

2 — *Careers*: Now, think about the careers that pay enough to afford that kind of lifestyle. — **3**

3 — *Education*: Start researching the kinds of education those careers require you to have in order to be successful. — **2**

4 — *School*: Now you are ready to start looking at schools that can give you the kind of education you need for your path! — **1**

About BeSeenSports™

Our mission is to help you create a robust picture of your academic and athletic career. BeSeenSports™ helps you to showcase your abilities on and off the field to college coaches all over the nation.

We provide you a complete website where you can flaunt your academic and athletic career. This website gives you specific pages for athletics, academics, your picture and video gallery and more! Your BeSeenSports&trade profile is all about you and no one else. The idea is to stand out from the competition, not increase it.

▶ Build Your Career

BeSeenSports™ is a powerful information management and marketing platform enabling student-athletes to highlight and market their skills in an entirely new way. More than just a single, muted page, BeSeenSports™ users have a more expanded profile. Allowing them to take control of their identity and moving from single dimensional profiles to a more in-depth website and online brand.

▶ Promote Your Brand

Taking your athletic career to the collegiate level takes a lot of work and dedication on and off the field. Coaches are looking for good players to consider. They are seeking student-athletes that will benefit their programs. BeSeenSports™ helps you to create an online focal point so everything about your academic and athletic career is located in a single location. Making it easy for them to see who you are.

▶ Exemplify Yourself

Exemplify your academic and athletic career by creating an essay that highlights everything you bring to the table and explains how a school and program can benefit from having you on their team! An exemplification letter describes why you are head and shoulders above the rest. When done well, it sets the tone for your live interviews.

BESEENSPORTS™

Get on the Radar!

BeSeenSports.com

My Notes: